IMAGES
of America

DETROIT
OPERA HOUSE

THE HOUSE THAT DAVID BUILT, 1993. Little did David DiChiera, founder and general director of Michigan Opera Theatre (MOT), realize when MOT purchased this dilapidated theater that it would become the catalyst for the revitalization of Detroit's sports and entertainment district. (Courtesy Michigan Opera Theatre.)

ON THE COVER: CROWDS LINE UP FOR WXYZ'S RADIO SCHOOLHOUSE PROGRAM, 1946. Each week, 40 juveniles were selected for this talent showcase, with 10 selected for solo spots and 30 for choral harmony. Groups of 10 rotated, so each had a solo spot at least once a month. (Courtesy Jan Kaulins Photography.)

IMAGES
of America

DETROIT
OPERA HOUSE

Michael Hauser and Marianne Weldon
Introduction by Lisa DiChiera

ARCADIA
PUBLISHING

Copyright © 2022 by Michael Hauser and Marianne Weldon
ISBN 978-1-4671-0777-8

Published by Arcadia Publishing
Charleston, South Carolina

Library of Congress Control Number: 2021948443

For all general information, please contact Arcadia Publishing:
Telephone 843-853-2070
Fax 843-853-0044
E-mail sales@arcadiapublishing.com
For customer service and orders:
Toll-Free 1-888-313-2665

Visit us on the Internet at www.arcadiapublishing.com

*Dedicated to the individual donors and major corporations
and foundations that believed in this project, and to the over
300 men and women who labored over the restoration of
this magnificent venue so future generations could enjoy
the arts thanks to the dream of David DiChiera.*

CONTENTS

ACKNOWLEDGMENTS

We greatly acknowledge the assistance of the following: American Classic Images, Broadway in Detroit, Mark Bowden at the Burton Historical Collection of the Detroit Public Library, Mitty Carter Photography, Central Business District Foundation, Continental Dining Management, Jeremy Dimick at the Detroit Historical Museum, Detroit Free Press Archives, Detroit News Archives, Cristina DiChiera, Lisa M. DiChiera, Jeff Garland Photography, Greenstone's Jewelry, John Grigaitis, Albert Kahn Collaborative, Jan Kaulins Photography, Del Kerney, James Luzenski, Alyn Thomas at Manning Brothers Historical Collection, Michigan Opera Theatre, Glen Calvin Moon, Jon Rosemond, Bryce Rudder, Theatre Historical Society, United Detroit Theatres Archives, Walsh College, Walter P. Reuther Library at Wayne State University, and our wonderful title manager, Caroline (Anderson) Vickerson.

INTRODUCTION

When David DiChiera moved from his hometown of Los Angeles to the Detroit area in 1962 after accepting a music professor position at the newly created Michigan State University–Oakland (today's Oakland University), his family and friends thought he had lost his mind. After completing a master's in composition and a doctorate in musicology at the University of California, Los Angeles (UCLA), he could have established himself as an esteemed academic at any major university in the country.

DiChiera had a hunch that by taking a job at a five-year-old university he could create innovative programs in opera, composition, and classical performance that went beyond typical academic study. In addition to teaching, he could produce vocal performances of both popular and lesser-known operas in the repertoire. DiChiera helped develop Oakland University's music department (today's School of Music, Theatre, and Dance) and helped launch its Meadow Brook Music Festival in 1964.

In 1963, DiChiera accepted the invitation of the Detroit Grand Opera Association (DGOA), the organization that brought the Metropolitan Opera national tour to Detroit each spring from 1959 through 1985, to direct its educational program, Overture to Opera, then producing opera previews around the city. DiChiera expanded the program to include full opera performances in English in locations ranging from the Detroit Institute of Arts to local high schools, with performers from Detroit and beyond. Believing that the nation's fifth largest city merited its own opera production company in addition to its art museum and symphony, he approached DGOA leadership with his vision. He won their support. An opera company was organized and funded as a division within DGOA under DiChiera's leadership. It produced its first full season in 1971. With its viability well established by 1971, the company became a fully independent organization, Michigan Opera Theatre (MOT).

While many of Detroit's businesses and residents fled to the suburbs in the 1970s, DiChiera firmly believed cultural institutions belonged in the city center. MOT's residency at Music Hall and the establishment of the Music Hall Center for the Performing Arts helped secure the surrounding business district, which included galleries and restaurants in adjacent Harmonie Park, and helped bring new life back to the neighboring Detroit Athletic Club (DAC). By 1984, MOT had seen enormous growth in budget and size of productions and needed larger stage and back-of-house space in order to produce grand opera. It was determined a new home was necessary in order for MOT to establish itself as an opera company of national prominence. In 1985, the last year of the Met's annual spring tour to Detroit, MOT took temporary residency at Detroit's Fisher Theatre for its fall season and the Masonic Temple for its spring season while looking for a permanent home. In MOT's 1987–1988 season program book, DiChiera's welcome statement read, "we must search for a permanent home, an opera house, either new or renovated, which can appropriately support the diverse repertory and activities that characterize a great opera company."

The story goes that in 1988, DiChiera's father-in-law and MOT board member Robert VanderKloot suggested DiChiera look at the ruinous Grand Circus Theatre, originally built as the Capitol Theatre in 1922, which was down the street from the Music Hall and across from Grand Circus Park. The former movie palace turned jazz venue turned B-movie house turned rock venue was now vacant and fast deteriorating. Members at the DAC were getting anxious about its appearance, and it had been discussed at a DAC board meeting to complain to the city. VanderKloot thought DiChiera and the MOT board should act fast. And in VanderKloot's opinion, remembering his early days of attending films there, the inside looked like a European opera house! DiChiera, MOT board chairman Robert Dewar, and several board members toured the building and agreed it looked like an opera house, and the size, with the exception of the stage house, was ideal. After months of negotiations with the owner, the historic theater was purchased in 1989 for $250,000. Now in possession of real estate and after completing condition and design analysis, a capital campaign was launched, chaired by Ford Motor Company president Philip Benton. The target was $20 million to both renovate the theater and demolish the adjacent Robert's Furs Building to make way for a larger stage house with state-of-the-art wing space, adequate stage depth, orchestra pit, dressing room accommodations, and loading dock.

DiChiera also made it a personal goal to provide comfortable seating (reducing the seat count from almost 4,000 to 2,700) and plenty of toilet stalls in the ladies room.

On October 13, 1991, Luciano Pavarotti was scheduled to perform an encore concert for MOT at Joe Louis Arena to kick off the 21st season. DiChiera convinced his friend to tour the dilapidated Grand Circus Theatre to show the legendary opera star his dream of creating an opera house for Detroit.

DiChiera later often told the story of touring Pavarotti through the building, cautioning him where not to walk on the deteriorated stage for fear of him falling through. Pavarotti projected a few notes into the auditorium from the stage and told DiChiera, "Yes, I think this will be a very nice opera house. I will come when it is completed." Never wanting to lose a promotional opportunity, DiChiera quickly had his staff organize a press conference in the theater where Pavarotti was able to publicly make the promise to return for a grand opening. This gave the campaign the boost it needed.

For the next six years, DiChiera and his wife Karen, the MOT board, capital campaign committee, and staff successfully raised the necessary funds that allowed the building, while not yet fully restored, to be "opera-able." On April 21, 1996, a star-studded grand opening was held, with a gala concert led by Pavarotti with legendary soprano Dame Joan Sutherland on hand to cut the red ribbon on the inaugurated stage with DiChiera and Dewar. Film actor and opera lover Roddy McDowall and singer/actor Ron Raines were masters of ceremonies. The event, attended by celebrities, political dignitaries, and loyal opera and theater lovers alike, made Detroit proud.

The Detroit Opera House for 25 years has been home to MOT's opera productions, educational programs such as Learning at the Opera House, the MOT Children's Choir, dance, concerts, and touring Broadway productions. In May 2018, at a grand salute in DiChiera's honor, MOT gave the Detroit Opera House the honorary name of the David DiChiera Center for the Performing Arts, announced on stage by Mayor Mike Duggan and former mayor Dennis Archer. In September 2018, DiChiera's memorial was held in the auditorium. It was his final act in the house that David built.

—Lisa M. DiChiera

The Capitol Theatre, today's Detroit Opera House, is a contributing building to the Grand Circus Park Historic District listed in the National Register of Historic Places in 1983 for its significance in architecture, theater, and community planning. The Detroit Opera House is eligible for individual listing in the National Register in the areas of Entertainment/Recreation and Architecture, but as of this publication has not been individually listed.

—Michigan State Historic Preservation Office

One

THE CAREFREE 1920s

BROADWAY ENTRANCE TO THE CAPITOL THEATRE, 1922. The "showplace of Michigan" adopted a policy for showcasing highly promoted live musical and dance performances to complement first-run feature films. *Peacock Alley* was a silent film from MGM featuring popular actress Mae Murray, who was also a dancer, producer, and screenwriter. (Courtesy Manning Brothers Historical Collection.)

C. Howard Crane, Architect Extraordinaire, 1922. Plans for the Capitol Theatre were drawn up by Crane and his associates, Elmer George Kiehler and Cyril C. Schley. Crane's firm was one of the foremost theater design studios, with offices in Detroit, Chicago, New York, London, and Paris. The firm designed over 250 venues, with 50 of them in Detroit alone. (Courtesy Michigan Opera Theatre.)

John Kunsky, Theater Impresario, 1922. Kunsky is credited with opening the first commercial motion picture theater in Michigan. In 1922, he added to his growing portfolio of venues with the addition of the Capitol, cited as being Detroit's first theater built in true movie palace style. Kunsky's managerial team included attorney and general manager George Trendle and advertising and stage production manager Howard O. Pierce. (Courtesy Walter P. Reuther Library, Wayne State University.)

EDUARD WERNER, DIRECTOR OF CAPITOL WONDER ORCHESTRA, 1922. Werner was a young Austrian immigrant whom Kunsky met in 1913 when he was a violinist at a Greenwich Village eatery. Kunsky brought him to Detroit to lead the Capitol Orchestra, 40 musicians culled from the Capitol and Madison Theatres. Besides performing overtures and film accompaniments, Werner also designed musical novelties that featured local artists. (Courtesy Detroit News Archives.)

MARGUERITE WERNER AT THE MIGHTY WURLITZER PIPE ORGAN, 1929. Eduard Werner's wife, Marguerite, was one of the nation's top solo organists. They met when both were appearing on stage at the neighboring Madison Theatre. This demonstration image depicts the new Wurlitzer Publix 1 console without ornamentation. This unit was waiting to be installed while the venue's original Hilgreen Lane pipe organ was being removed. (Courtesy Walter P. Reuther Library, Wayne State University.)

11

THE MIGHTY WURLITZER PIPE ORGAN AT THE CAPITOL, 1929. This unit was installed in 1929 and was the first Publix 1 manufactured by Wurlitzer. The purchase price was reportedly $47,000. The Wurlitzer replaced the 3/38 Hilgreen Lane pipe organ, which was installed in 1921. Following years of little use, this Wurlitzer was removed in 1957 to Detroit's Arcadia Roller Rink. After passing through several additional owners, in 1972, it was donated to the Paramount Theatre in Oakland, California. (Courtesy Theatre Historical Society.)

THE CAPITOL SUNDAY CONCERTS, 1925. Eduard Werner led Detroit's first motion picture theater symphony orchestra at the Capitol. The concerts featured 75 musicians and were staged each Sunday at noon, following worship services. Admission was 75¢, and patrons could stay for the feature film at no additional charge. These concerts drew sell-out audiences from 1922 until 1926, when Werner moved to Kunsky's newly opened Michigan Theatre. (Both, courtesy Michael Hauser.)

J.L. Hudson Co. Concert Band at the Capitol, 1922. The nearby Hudson's Department Store at one time had its own 25-member concert band and quartet. In September 1922, the band was featured on the stage of the Capitol for a weeklong engagement to celebrate the store's 41st anniversary. It accompanied the Capitol's own orchestra for all matinee and evening performances that week. Jack LaMoth (inset) was a former member of Hudson's band prior to joining the Capitol Orchestra. (Both, courtesy Michael Hauser.)

Dress Rehearsal for a Stage Presentation, 1927. Typical live appearances in the 1920s would include an orchestra overture, a pipe organ solo, and a musical performance with singers and dancers and occasional appearances from film stars. Elaborate Publix stage productions from Paramount Pictures ran from January to August 1926 at the Capitol and then moved over to the newly opened Michigan Theatre. (Courtesy Manning Brothers Historical Collection.)

BROADWAY STREET EXTERIOR OF THE CAPITOL, 1922. Ground was broken for the Capitol on April 5, 1921, with the complex consisting of the theater and two attached office buildings occupying three parcels of land. One of the conditions of the original 99-year lease to Kunsky stipulated that the theater be constructed in such a manner that if it failed, the land would revert to the owners and each would have a separate building on their respective properties. (Courtesy Manning Brothers Historical Collection.)

CRAFTSMANSHIP CONSTRUCTING THE CAPITOL, 1927. It took Kunsky and Trendle two years of negotiations with 12 property owners to acquire the site. The final cost to construct the theater and the adjacent office buildings was $2.75 million, equivalent to $28 million today. To construct the Capitol took 5,560,000 pounds of cement, 7,000 yards of sand, 50,000 partition tiles, 300,000 face bricks, and 1,000 yards of pipe. (Courtesy Manning Brothers Historical Collection.)

THE CAPITOL, "DETROIT'S FOREMOST PLAYHOUSE," 1923. This theater formally opened on January 12, 1922, with several thousand guests waiting in sub-freezing temperatures to gain entrance. The program that evening included the Capitol Orchestra playing the *1812 Overture*, soloist Estelle Carey, the Capitol grand pipe organ, the Capitol mixed quartette, a Pathé newsreel, Pathé Education Review, and Snub Pollard comedy, and the John Barrymore silent film *The Lotus Eater*. (Courtesy Manning Brothers Historical Collection.)

LONG LINES FOR COMEDY AT THE CAPITOL, 1926. Guests line up for the Paramount silent comedy *Hands Up*, starring Raymond Griffith, one of the most popular comedians at that time. The three buildings depicted at Witherell Street between Madison Avenue and Broadway Street were demolished for parking, and in later years, the new stagehouse for what is now the Detroit Opera House was constructed on this site. (Courtesy Manning Brothers Historical Collection.)

BROADWAY STREET EXTERIOR OF THE CAPITOL, 1927. The original plan for the Capitol called for 4,250 seats but was modified to 3,400. Staffing, besides management, included the orchestra, singers, several hundred ushers, a fulltime music librarian, a fulltime master scenic artist, a maintenance team, and a sign painter. Shortly after opening, the venue also started screening newsreels from both the *Detroit News* and the *Detroit Free Press*. (Courtesy Manning Brothers Historical Collection.)

MADISON AVENUE FACADE OF THE CAPITOL, 1929. Despite the fact that the Madison Avenue facade was not as inviting as the Broadway Street facade, this entrance for many years was the carriage trade entrance. Note the "cooled by refrigeration" sign above the doors. Movie theaters were among the first buildings to feature air-conditioning. "Del is back" referred to the revered band leader Del Delbridge, who appeared in over 1,500 performances at the Capitol between 1922 and 1930. (Courtesy Manning Brothers Historical Collection.)

THE CAPITOL BECOMES THE PARAMOUNT THEATRE, 1929. From August 1929 through December 1932, this venue was owned and operated by the Publix Theatre division of Paramount Pictures. With the oncoming Depression, Publix desperately tried to make this venue profitable via promotions that included complimentary tickets, dishes, coffee, and even free gum! It was actually less expensive to keep the theater closed in 1933 and 1934. Publix sold the venue back to Kunsky in 1934. (Courtesy Manning Brothers Historical Collection.)

BROADWAY STREET LOBBY, 1929. The Broadway Street lobby for most of this venue's life has been the main entrance. From the 1920s through the 1940s, most patrons arrived via several streetcar lines that stopped at these doors. Up to 35,000 guests a day would enter via this lobby. Today, the majority of guests park in the adjacent Detroit Opera House parking center. Aside from the brass rails, this lobby, following its restoration, is virtually unchanged. (Courtesy Manning Brothers Historical Collection.)

BROADWAY STREET BOX OFFICE, 1922. Despite the size of this theater, the box office was relatively compact. The exterior is surrounded by marble, decorative plaster, and red damask velvet curtains. Today, there are three guest service stations, and for the restoration, historic images were consulted to retain the original color palate for the plaster and walls and the design of the draperies. (Courtesy Manning Brothers Historical Collection.)

AUDITORIUM LOOKING BACK TO THE GRAND LOBBY FROM THE STAGE, 1929. This image provides an idea of the expanse of the auditorium, depicting main-floor seating, box-level seats, and the mezzanine and balcony. The ceiling dome is 65 feet in diameter and was originally ringed with 3,000 multicolored incandescent lightbulbs. Note also the original projection booth and the spotlight booth. (Courtesy Manning Brothers Historical Collection.)

SIDE VIEW OF THE CAPITOL AUDITORIUM, 1922. The auditorium features intricate plaster reliefs in many shapes and sizes. The large oval grilles on both sides hid the many pipes for the pipe organ that was situated house right. The theater was built without sound amplification for vaudeville acts, thus the acoustics have proven to be excellent for today's productions. The first talking picture to play the Capitol was Paramount's *Warming Up*, starring Richard Dix. (Courtesy Manning Brothers Historical Collection.)

THE CAPITOL'S STAGE PROSCENIUM, 1929. The plaster proscenium panels surrounding the stage feature renderings of historic Detroit buildings, the scales of justice, tools of the trowel trades, and whimsical theatrical images. During the years of abandonment in the 1980s, most of these panels were damaged and had to be repaired or new casts created in the plaster shops set up in the auditorium. (Courtesy Manning Brothers Historical Collection.)

OVERVIEW OF THE AUDITORIUM FROM THE BALCONY, 1929. This expansive view illustrates the depth of the auditorium. The orchestra pit could accommodate 40 musicians, and the pipe organ was located house right. Note the chandeliers in front of the pipe organ grilles on each side of the auditorium as well as the tall torchieres leading up to the stage. There are five large plaster sunbursts above the proscenium. (Courtesy Manning Brothers Historical Collection.)

LOOKING UP AT THE BOX LEVEL FROM THE MAIN FLOOR, 1922. The box level features subdued lighting, and many guests miss the beauty of this area of the theater. The ceiling contains hundreds of plaster rosettes in gold and sky blue tones interspersed with large milk glass light fixtures that feature intricate cast iron designs. For privacy, originally each box had heavy green drapery hung from brass rods at the rear. Today, because the theater is a live performance venue, walls and doors have been added. (Courtesy Manning Brothers Historical Collection.)

CLOSE-UP OF TORCHIERE BASE IN THE AUDITORIUM, 1922. Four plaster torchieres flank both sides of the auditorium leading up to the stage. All of them sustained damage during the years the venue was abandoned and had to be restored. Each one provides ambient light to create a moody feeling. (Courtesy Michigan Opera Theatre.)

VIEW OF THE GRAND LOBBY, 1929. The foyer of the grand lobby extends over 200 feet from the Broadway Street entrance to the Madison Avenue entrance. The back of the auditorium is open with a wood spindle base flanked with a plate glass wall. The poster at the top of the staircase promotes MGM's *Wonder of Woman*, a "pre-code" drama released before enforcement of the Motion Picture Production Code. (Courtesy Manning Brothers Historical Collection.)

CLOSER LOOK AT THE GRAND STAIRCASE, 1929. The grand staircase is one of the most popular spots in the theater to be seen. The cast iron design of the rails includes rosettes and the Capitol crest. C. Howard Crane, the venue's architect, loved rosettes, which can also be found on ceilings throughout the theater. Plaster images to the left of the staircase include griffins, serpents, rams' heads, and cupids. Note the heavy drapery providing privacy for the boxes on this level. (Courtesy Manning Brothers Historical Collection.)

AN EYE-CATCHING VIEW OF THE GRAND LOBBY, 1929. The signature of the grand lobby is the three enormous chandeliers. Each of these light fixtures depicts an overflowing fruit cup with grapes and grape leaves at the top surrounded by pears and plums and a pineapple representing friendship at the base. There are over 3,000 pieces of Czechoslovakian cut crystal in each fixture. (Courtesy Manning Brothers Historical Collection.)

REVEALING ART IN THE SHADOWS OF THE GRAND LOBBY, 1929. Kunsky's inspiration for the Capitol was his visits to European opera houses and images of the Villa Medama and the Vatican. He spent two years procuring the oil paintings that were originally placed in the foyers and lounges. (Courtesy Manning Brothers Historical Collection.)

RICH MILK GLASS CEILING LIGHTS, 1922. These intricate light fixtures were incorporated into ceilings in both the main-floor auditorium and the second-floor box level. The designs within each fixture are cast iron. Many of these were stolen during the abandoned years of the 1980s, and Michigan Opera Theatre had to purchase a number of them back from out-of-state antique dealers. (Courtesy Manning Brothers Historical Collection.)

THE GENTLEMEN'S SMOKING LOUNGE, 1929. This lounge is on the lower level of the theater beneath the grand staircase. For many years, patrons were allowed to smoke in the balcony, thus this room featured both ashtrays and spittoons for those who chewed tobacco. The clubroom feel of this lounge includes a decorative fireplace, leaded-glass windows, and relaxing leather chairs. (Courtesy Manning Brothers Historical Collection.)

ORIGINAL LADIES' POWDER ROOM ON THE BOX LEVEL, 1922. This intimate area on the second level was strictly for women to powder their noses. It was furnished in a style known then as Chinese Chippendale and featured a large Oriental rug, Asian tapestries, Asian-inspired light fixtures, and pagodas atop the two large mirrors. (Courtesy Manning Brothers Historical Collection.)

Two

THE CHALLENGING 1930S
AND THE 1940S WAR YEARS

A QUIET RESPITE ON THE BOX LEVEL, 1937. This image provides a closer look at the Chinese Chippendale style of decor in the ladies' powder room, which includes various detailed wall fabrics and tapestries. This area provided a pay telephone station and two sets of stairs for access to balcony seating. (Courtesy Manning Brothers Historical Collection.)

Capitol Theatre

(Formerly Paramount)

DETROIT CONCERT SOCIETY

ISOBEL J. HURST, Director

P R E S E N T S

SAN CARLO
OPERA COMPANY

FORTUNE GALLO, General Director

COMPANY OF 150
San Carlo Opera Ballet

Presenting a repertoire of world-famous operas by casts of
of notables from the great music temples of the world.

CARLO PERONI, Musical Director　LUIGI RAYBAUT, Stage Director

AIDA
Sunday Evening, October 6, at 8:20

Aida	Bianca Saroya
Amneris	Dreda Aves
Radames	Aroldo Lindi
Amonasro	Mostyn Thomas
Ramfis	Harold Kravitt
King of Egypt	Natale Cervi
A Messenger	Francesco Curci
Priestess	Charlotte Bruno

LA TOSCA
Monday Evening, October 7, at 8:20

Floria Tosca (A Celebrated Songstress)	Goeta Ljungberg (Guest)
Baron Scarpia (Chief of Police)	Mario Valle
Mario Cavaradossi (A Painter)	Dimitri Onofrei
Spoletta (A Police Agent)	Francesco Curci
Sciarrone (A Gendarme)	Fausto Bozza
Cesare Angelotti (A Political Prisoner)	Harold Kravitt
A Sacristan	Natalie Cervi
A Jailer	Fausto Bozza
A Shepherd Boy	Charlotte Bruno

CARMEN
Tuesday Evening, October 8, at 8:20

Carmen	Dreda Aves
Don Jose	Aroldo Lindi
Escamillo	Mostyn Thomas
Micaela	Charlotte Simons
Dancairo	Natalie Cervi
Zuniga	Harold Kravitt
Remendado	Francesco Curci
Morales	Robert Scott
Frasquita	Philine Falco
Mercedes	Charlotte Bruno

FAUST
Wednesday Evening, October 9, at 8:20

Marguerite	Charlotte Simons
Faust	Rolph Gerard
Mephistopheles	Harold Kravitt
Valentine	Mario Valle
Siebel	Charlotte Bruno
Wagner	Robert Scott
Martha	Philine Falco

CAVALLERIA RUSTICANA
Thursday Evening, October 10, at 8:20

Santuzza	Bianca Saroya
Lola	Charlotte Bruno
Mamma Lucia	Philine Falco
Faust	Rolf Gerard
Alfio	Stefan Kozakevich

FOLLOWED BY

OPERA AT THE BROADWAY CAPITOL, 1930s. Between the late 1920s and mid-1930s, live opera was presented on the stage of this venue during its years as both the Paramount and Broadway Capitol. San Carlo was a touring grand opera company of over 100 artists founded by the Italian American impresario Fortune Gallo. The theater would halt films for a week while San Carlo performed a different opera on stage each day with local talent paired with the traveling troupe. (Courtesy Michael Hauser.)

CELEBRITY CRUSH ON BROADWAY, 1930. This image captures the excitement of crowds storming the Capitol to see Peggy Hopkins Joyce, a blonde 1920s film star and former Ziegfeld Follies performer who became famous for marrying wealthy gentlemen. Note the onlookers at windows and others trying to catch a glimpse from their vehicles. (Courtesy Burton Historical Collection, Detroit Public Library.)

A QUIET AFTERNOON ON BROADWAY, 1945. This view captures the tall Capitol blade sign from two blocks away. Several Department of Street Railways (DSR) streetcars stopped at the Capitol's front doors. From the 1920s through the 1940s, up to 35,000 guests a day would enter through these doors to enjoy films, listen to the Capitol Orchestra, or attend a stage presentation. (Courtesy Manning Brothers Historical Collection.)

A View of the Broadway Street Lobby, 1931. The area above the storm lobby doors was reserved for promoting upcoming films. These custom posters were designed by the venue's in-house sign painter. This one was for MGM's *New Moon*, a pre-code romantic melodrama starring Grace Moore and Lawrence Tibbett. (Courtesy Manning Brothers Historical Collection.)

MGM Stages a World Premiere at the Paramount, 1931. The studio generated much publicity for the premiere of *Free Soul*, starring Norma Shearer, with klieg lights, enhanced marquee signage, and a band. This was an American pre-code drama that also starred Lionel Barrymore, Clark Gable, and Leslie Howard. The promotional tagline for the film screamed: "She's free with love—free with kisses, living life like a man!" (Courtesy United Detroit Theatres Archives.)

THE PARAMOUNT IN ALL OF ITS GLORY, 1931. The six-story Paramount blade sign practically dwarfs the theater. The Publix arm of the studio retained the cantilevered marquee, making only minor modifications. *Strangers May Kiss*, the featured film, was an MGM pre-code drama starring Norma Shearer and Robert Montgomery. (Courtesy Manning Brothers Historical Collection.)

LINING UP FOR A SUNDAY MATINEE, 1941. Generations of families made it a tradition to attend Sunday matinees, especially if the show included a double feature. This image shows a crowd attending two sea pictures from Warner Bros.: *The Sea Hawk* with Errol Flynn and *The Sea Wolf* with Edward G. Robinson. (Courtesy United Detroit Theatres Archives.)

USHERETTES AT THE BROADWAY CAPITOL, 1942. A breakthrough for female employment in film exhibition occurred as a result of the manpower shortage during World War II. Aside from usherettes, the Broadway Capitol was one of the first venues to employ a female manager. United Detroit Theatres (UDT), owner of the venue, had a definitive policy for hiring female managers that was backed with an extensive training program. (Courtesy Del Kerney.)

MARKETING AND PUBLIC RELATIONS DYNAMO, 1940s. Alice Gorham joined United Detroit Theatres in 1934 as a copywriter and by 1939 was its director of advertising and public relations. Gorham worked on many campaigns for films that premiered at the Broadway Capitol. She was one of the highest ranking and most respected females in the motion picture business and received many accolades and awards from national organizations. (Courtesy United Detroit Theatres Archives.)

HOLLYWOOD
WAR BOND
CAVALCADE
OF STARS

S
T
A
F
F

1943

WAR BOND PREMIERES IN THE 1940s. Hudson's Department Store and movie theaters sold more bonds for the war effort than anyone else. A war bond premiere would include a preview of a new studio film, an appearance by one of the film's stars, an orchestra, and several singers. The program would be broadcast on all local radio stations. (Both, courtesy United Detroit Theatres Archives.)

CROWDS LINE UP FOR *RADIO SCHOOLHOUSE*, 1946. For several decades, the Broadway Capitol was the place to be on Sunday afternoons. WXYZ radio broadcast *Radio Schoolhouse* from the stage, hosted by radio personality Dick Osgood. The talent showcase was similar to today's *The Voice*. Part of the allure was prize money given away each week. (Courtesy Jan Kaulins Photography.)

4TH WAR LOAN RETAIL RALLY

THIS TIME IT'S INDOORS AT THE

FOX, MICHIGAN AND CAPITOL THEATRES

TUESDAY MORNING - - JANUARY, 11th

9:15 a.m. - - - Doors Open at 9:00 a.m.

Principal Downtown Stores Will Open at 10:45 a.m.
To Permit Your Attendance — Shows Over by 10:30

WAR LOAN RALLY AT THE BROADWAY CAPITOL, 1944. Early-morning war loan rallies were held at the Broadway Capitol as well as other downtown theaters. Special trailers shown with each feature encouraged patrons to purchase war bonds in the lobby, night and day. There were even free movie days for those who purchased war bonds. (Courtesy Michael Hauser.)

NATIONAL SCREEN SERVICE

CORPORATION

── PRE ‑ VUES + ACCESSORIES ──

Herman Robbins, President

Jack G. Leo, Vice-Pres. & Treas.

630 NINTH AVENUE, NEW YORK 19, N. Y.

Branches:

Albany
Atlanta
Boston
Buffalo
Charlotte
Chicago
Cincinnati
Cleveland
Dallas
Denver
Des Moines
Detroit
Indianapolis
Kansas City
Los Angeles
Memphis
Milwaukee
Minneapolis
New Haven
New Orleans
New York
Oklahoma City
Omaha
Philadelphia
Pittsburgh
Portland
St. Louis
Salt Lake City
San Francisco
Seattle
Washington

Studios:

Hollywood
New York

November 16, 1944

To: ALL BRANCH MANAGERS

SIXTH WAR LOAN EDDIE BRACKEN TRAILER

"A MESSAGE OF IMPORTANCE"

The second trailer on the Sixth War Loan, starring
Eddie Bracken, entitled "A MESSAGE OF IMPORTANCE",
will be shipped to you in the same quantities as
you received on the Jennifer Jones Sixth War Loan
trailer.

Your allotment of the Eddie Bracken trailer, which
measures approximately 180 ft. in length, should
arrive in your exchange on or about November 28th.

SIXTH WAR LOAN RECORDS: Please refer to my letter
of November 8th relative to the Sixth War Loan
record - Buy A Bond Today" ... "What Kind Of An
American Are You?". These records are now being
shipped to all branches individually packed and not
part in bulk.

SMASH 'EM WITH THE SIXTH!

Donald L. Velde

DLV:DS

War Loan Trailers Helped Sell War Bonds, 1944. Regular correspondence to theater owners and managers from the National Screen Service kept the Broadway Capitol stocked with up-to-date trailers to be shown prior to each feature. The service also provided lobby posters, banners, and heralds for the ushers to distribute to patrons. (Courtesy Michael Hauser.)

Three

THE BOOMING 1950S AND THE SWINGING 1960S

TOP BRASS IN THE UDT SCREENING ROOM, 1950S. The Broadway Capitol was part of the United Detroit Theatres circuit, the largest and most prestigious local chain of theaters. UDT had its own screening room on the 16th floor of the former Stroh Building on Grand Circus Park. Here, executives of UDT would screen films in advance to determine how successful a picture would be and which theater to book the film into. (Courtesy United Detroit Theatres Archives.)

DIVERSE ENTERTAINMENT IN THE 1950S. United Detroit Theatres leased the Broadway Capitol from 1950 to 1954 to local independent exhibitor Saul Korman, who energized the venue with a 24-hour policy. Korman booked big band names like Lionel Hampton and Duke Ellington, jazz on the weekends, and a steady diet of horror films such as the world premiere of *Creature from the Black Lagoon* in 1952. (Courtesy United Detroit Theatres Archives.)

A PACKED HOUSE FOR RADIO STATION BROADCASTS, 1950S. WXYZ began broadcasting radio programs direct from the stage of the Broadway Capitol in 1936. Initially, these broadcasts would include an orchestra, an opera singer, and several soloists. The success of these productions paved the way for WXYZ's *Radio Schoolhouse* talent showcase as well as lobby broadcasts for film premieres. (Courtesy United Detroit Theatres Archives.)

SALUTE TO WOMEN WHO WORK EVENT, 1954. This annual event was coordinated by the Central Business District Foundation to highlight the importance of females in the workplace. Mary Morgan from CKLW, known locally as "the most beautiful woman in radio," was the master of ceremonies. The event also included a sales chat and fashion show. (Courtesy Central Business District Foundation.)

★ THEATRE GUEST TICKET ★

Downtown Detroit Days

OCTOBER 17 - 18 - 19

—— Good on Above Days for ——

One Guest Admission

Between 10:45 A.M. and Closing

— at —

**ADAMS • FOX • MADISON
MICHIGAN • PALMS
BROADWAY CAPITOL • TELENEWS**

64

SUPPORTING VARIOUS PROMOTIONS, 1950s. The Broadway Capitol and the other United Detroit Theatres downtown were strong supporters of the semiannual Downtown Detroit Days. Guest tickets were provided to the Central Business District Foundation as part of prize packages. This was also a great way to promote upcoming new films in Downtown Detroit Days ad supplements and brochures. (Both, courtesy Central Business District Foundation.)

SALES SEMINAR

"A Salute to Women Who Work in Detroit"

WEDNESDAY, MARCH 14, 1956
BROADWAY CAPITOL THEATRE
9:00 - 10:00 A.M.

Sponsored by
THE CENTRAL BUSINESS DISTRICT ASSOCIATION

PERSONAL APPEARANCE BY CLAYTON MOORE, THE LONE RANGER, 1958. George Trendle, president of United Detroit Theatres (and owner of the Broadway Capitol), was also in the radio business and created *The Lone Ranger*, which began as a radio program prior to being franchised to motion pictures and television. Here, Moore is in the Broadway Capitol lobby promoting the opening of Warner Bros.' *The Lost City of Gold*. (Courtesy Detroit Free Press Archives.)

THE FILM THAT WOULD NOT GO AWAY, 1959. The controversial *Uncle Tom's Cabin* was initially released by Universal Pictures as a silent film in 1927. It is based on the 1852 novel by Harriet Beecher Stowe. In 1958, this film was rereleased with added sound and narrated by well-known actor Raymond Massey. This film continuously made the rounds of all downtown theaters when they needed a filler well into the early 1980s. (Courtesy United Detroit Theatres Archives.)

HEARTTHROB SAL MINEO: A CROWD PLEASER AT THE BROADWAY CAPITOL, 1950S. The Broadway Capitol hosted several premieres of films in which Sal Mineo starred and appeared in person on stage. Mineo at this time was one of Hollywood's hottest stars and appeared in *The Young Don't Cry, Rock Pretty Baby, Dino,* and *The Gene Krupa Story,* all of which played successful runs at the Broadway Capitol. (Courtesy United Detroit Theatres Archives.)

WORLD SCREAMIERE OF *THE TINGLER*, 1959. Several of William Castle's films for Columbia Pictures had their world premieres at the Broadway Capitol. For *The Tingler*, which opened at midnight, the theater hosted a street party and costume contest. Almost 65,000 patrons attended the first week's run, and the premiere made Hollywood gossip columnist Hedda Hopper's column. (Courtesy Central Business District Foundation.)

EARLY ROCK AND ROLL SHOWS AT THE BROADWAY CAPITOL, 1960. Detroit's first rock and roll show was staged at the Broadway Capitol in 1954 and featured Bill Haley and the Comets. Various radio stations through the years would host a cavalcade of artists. This WQTE *Biggest Show of Stars* included Bobby Rydell, Bo Diddley, Chubby Checker, Sam Cooke, Dion and the Belmonts, the Bobbettes, Duane Eddy, Marv Johnson, and the Olympics all on the same bill. (Courtesy Michigan Opera Theatre.)

A New Chapter and a New Name for the Broadway Capitol, 1960. The Broadway Capitol closed in October 1959 for a six-figure, two-month makeover and a new name. The newly renamed Grand Circus Theatre received new seats, new carpeting, a new marquee, and new projection equipment. Helen Wilmore, a well-known designer, was brought in by United Detroit Theatres to design and oversee the renovation. (Courtesy United Detroit Theatres Archives.)

RETAIL TIE-INS WITH THE NEW NAME, 1960. This display at the House of Living Rooms in Royal Oak, Michigan, is one of many that appeared around town celebrating the renovation and name change of the Broadway Capitol. The opening film was Paramount's *The World of Suzie Wong*. Seating was reduced from 3,200 to 1,400 for a more comfortable and intimate guest experience. (Courtesy United Detroit Theatres Archives.)

UNITED DETROIT THEATRES CORPORATION

Operating the

MICHIGAN • PALMS • FISHER • MADISON • BROADWAY CAPITOL
CINDERELLA • MEL • VARSITY • VOGUE • RAMONA • NORWEST
BIRMINGHAM • BLOOMFIELD • WOODS

•

Executive Offices

28 WEST ADAMS AVENUE
TELEPHONE WOODWARD 3-4000
DETROIT 26. MICH.

December 15, 1960

Mr. Joseph Lee
Fox Theatre
2211 Woodward Avenue
Detroit 1, Michigan

Dear Joe:

Please pardon the informality of this invitation.

You are cordially invited to attend a special Preview Showing of
THE WORLD OF SUZIE WONG, starring William Holden and Nancy Kwan,
at 8:30 p.m. on Thursday evening, December 22, which occasion
will be our formal unveiling of the Grand Circus Theatre (just off
Grand Circus Park), Detroit's new luxury showplace for special top
quality film attractions.

Through the courtesy of the Detroit Athletic Club, which has engaged
the theatre for this occasion, we are able to invite you to be among
the first-night audience for this exciting event.

Enclosed please find two reserved seat tickets, which we sincerely
hope you will be able to use. Black tie apparel is optional.

Cordially yours,

W. R. PRAUGHT
President

WRP:jo

P.S. - Through arrangements with the Variety Club of Detroit,
the clubroom facilities will be open to preview guests
following the performance -- 14th Floor, Tuller Hotel.

OPENING NIGHT INVITATION FOR A REINVIGORATED VENUE, 1960. United Detroit Theatres was proud of its downtown venues, which included the Madison, the Palms, the Michigan, and the Grand Circus Theatres, and put its faith into Downtown Detroit by booking first-run pictures from the major studios. (Courtesy Michael Hauser.)

UNITED DETROIT THEATRES PARTNERS WITH THE CENTRAL BUSINESS DISTRICT ASSOCIATION, 1962. United Detroit Theatres partnered with the Central Business District Association for all of its important promotional events, such as Downtown Detroit Days, Mother's Day, Father's Day, and the Salute to Women Who Work Week. Promotions included special film screenings and complimentary tickets. (Courtesy Central Business District Foundation.)

GOING AFTER THE FEMALE CAREER MARKET, 1964. The Grand Circus participated in United Detroit Theatres' plan to boost attendance on Tuesdays, which traditionally was a slow day at the box office. People who worked downtown could attend a movie at a discounted price from opening to closing. A similar program was also instituted for young folks on Fridays and Saturdays. (Courtesy Central Business District Foundation.)

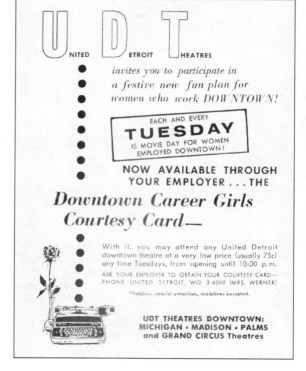

THE GRAND CIRCUS MARQUEE, 1964. This v-shaped marquee was installed in 1959 and was capable of 11 lines of copy. There were three different sizes of both red and blue plastic and metal letters. The marquee itself was metal with a porcelain finish, and was lit with 1,500 high-output fluorescent bulbs. Universal Pictures selected the Grand Circus for the world premiere of *McHale's Navy* in 1964. (Courtesy Jan Kaulins Photography.)

TWENTIETH CENTURY-FOX FILM CORPORATION

HEAD OFFICE 444 WEST 56TH STREET, NEW YORK, N.Y. 10019
BRANCHES IN ALL PRINCIPAL CITIES OF THE WORLD
2211 CASS AVENUE
DETROIT, MICH., 48201
TELEPHONE 313-WOODWARD 1-3726

12/29/65

Dear Sir:

You are cordially invited to attend a Sneak
Preview screening on "OUR MAN FLINT" at:

Grand Circus Theatre   1526 Broadway

8:00 P.M.   Sunday Evening   January 2, 1966

"OUR MAN FLINT" stars James Coburn and Lee J. Cobb,
in Cinemascope and Deluxe Color.

"OUR MAN FLINT" shapes up as a Super-spy thriller
of the unexpected and bizarre, with all the interest and
excitement created by recent films of international
intrigue.

This letter presented at the door will admit you
and a guest.

Kindest regards.

Sincerely,

F. Bunkelman

Fred Bunkelman

FB/eu

SNEAK PREVIEWS AT THE GRAND CIRCUS, 1965. The Grand Circus Theatre was frequently selected by major studios for sneak previews of coming attractions. Detroit was considered an excellent test market for the public's perception of new films. For exhibitors, the studios conducted advance screenings either at the Film Exchange Building on Cass Avenue or at United Detroit Theatres' screening room in the Stroh Building. (Courtesy Michael Hauser.)

THE GRAND LOBBY OF THE GRAND CIRCUS, 1967. Nicholas George Theatres, operators of primarily suburban venues, took a gamble on Downtown Detroit in the 1960s and 1970s by operating the Grand Circus, Michigan, and Plaza (former Telenews) Theatres in the Grand Circus Park theater district. As seen in this image, the grand lobby still projected an upscale appearance. (Courtesy Theatre Historical Society.)

Broadway Street Exterior of the Grand Circus, 1967. The Grand Circus scored an exclusive run of 20th Century Fox's *St. Valentine's Day Massacre* in 1967. United Detroit Theatres had terminated its lease on this theater in 1964, and Nicholas George Theatres took over from 1964 to 1966. In 1966, the theater was purchased from descendants of the original landowners by Community Theatres and Suburban Detroit Theatres. (Courtesy Theatre Historical Society.)

Four

THE TUMULTUOUS 1970S AND THE GENERATIONAL 1980S

A MOVIE VALUE SPREE!

Downtown **D**etroit **D**ays

Downtown
Detroit Theatres
welcome
DOWNTOWN DETROIT DAYS
Shoppers

This ticket presented at the **ADAMS, FOX, GRAND CIRCUS, MADISON, PALMS OR PLAZA** Theatres—any day, Mondays thru Thursdays inclusive, up to and including Thursday, March 9, 1978 will **ADMIT ONE ADULT**

FINAL DOWNTOWN DETROIT DAYS PROMOTION FOR THE GRAND CIRCUS, 1978. The days were numbered, and this was the final major promotion that the Grand Circus Theatre would participate in. The balcony, the mezzanine, and the box-level concession stand were closed, and many of the decorative light fixtures throughout the venue remained dark. (Courtesy Central Business District Foundation.)

EXTERIOR BEAUTIFICATION 1970S STYLE, 1971. In the early 1970s, the Grand Circus Theatre participated in a downtown art project funded by Detroit Renaissance and commissioned by Art for Detroit, a local nonprofit. A 2,400-square-foot mural on the north side of the theater was created by Aris Koutroulis, a professor at Wayne State University. He utilized 110 gallons of paint to create 60 lines in 15 colors around an open center. (Courtesy Detroit News Archives.)

DOUBLE FEATURE EXPLOITATION FLICKS, 1973. Throughout the 1970s, the Grand Circus stayed alive by screening all genre of exploitation films: horror, gore, Blaxploitation, and soft-core porn. Occasionally, the venue would be part of a multiple booking from one of the major studios. The all-time box office champ was Cinemations' *Sweet Sweetback's Baadasssss Song*, which in 1971 broke all house records and played here for an amazing 10 weeks. (Courtesy Theatre Historical Society.)

FILMS WITH AN EMPHASIS ON MUSIC, 1973. Music-oriented films in the 1970s such as *Lady Sings the Blues*, *Sparkle*, *Wattstax*, and *The Wiz* kept the doors to downtown venues including the Grand Circus open. Additional enticements included visits from the films' stars, swag items, and live radio broadcasts from the lobby. (Courtesy Michael Hauser.)

CHOP SOCKEY FILMS WERE MAJOR DRAWS, 1973. When the popularity of Blaxploitation films faded, downtown venues gravitated towards horror, gore, and kung-fu films to fill the seats. Warner Bros.' *Enter the Dragon*, starring Bruce Lee, grossed an astounding $75,000 during its debut week in 1974 at the Grand Circus. There was enough new product that all kung-fu bookings were double features. (Courtesy Michael Hauser.)

A WELL-WORN STAGE, 1977. Here is a close-up view of the line sets and Bull Dog Electrical Products light board on the stage. Both are original from 1922, when the theater featured daily live productions. They were also utilized for radio broadcasts, including WXYZ's *Radio Schoolhouse*, and during the rock concert era from 1981 to 1985. (Courtesy Detroit Free Press Archives.)

TRUSTING THE BABYSITTER, 1978. With an operating cost of $5,000 a week to break even, the Grand Circus on some weeks was not even approaching that, regardless of the booking. The last successful film at the box office was Universal's *Blue Collar*, which had premiered earlier in 1978. In November 1978, following the final screening of *Jailbait Babysitter*, this once-grand palace closed its doors as a film venue. (Courtesy Detroit Free Press Archives.)

THE BLUES BREAKERS IN CONCERT, 1982.
The initial publicist for Grand Circus Live!
was well-known Detroit entrepreneur Jerry
Shoenith. The switch to live entertainment
brought a smorgasbord of talent that included
comedians, mimes, sports figures, and a
myriad of musicians. By 1982, this evolved to
a steady parade of international rock artists.
(Courtesy American Classic Images.)

**ENGLISH ROCK BAND MOTORHEAD AS
DECEMBER HEADLINERS, 1982.** The year
1982 proved to be a bonanza for booking top-
name acts. The Grand Circus stage hosted
the Plasmatics, Spyrogyra, *Beatlemania!*, Rick
Springfield, the Ramones, the B-52's, Roberta
Flack, the Blues Breakers, the Clash, Steel
Pulse, Gang of Four, the Stray Cats, Bonnie
Raitt, Dr. John, Sippie Wallace, and a host of
others. (Courtesy Detroit Historical Society.)

METRO TIMES FIRST ANNUAL DETROIT MUSIC AWARDS, 1982. In November 1982, the Grand Circus hosted what would become an annual tradition: the Detroit Music Awards. This event coincided with the second anniversary of the *Metro Times*, Detroit's longstanding alternative weekly publication and a stalwart supporter of the local entertainment community. (Courtesy Michael Hauser.)

PLATINUM RIDERS TAKE TOP PRIZE AT AWARDS, 1982. Winners at the first Detroit Music Awards held at the Grand Circus included the Platinum Riders as best funk and rhythm and blues band, the Cadillac Kidz as best rock band, the Marcus Belgrave Group as best jazz combo, and the Sun Messengers as best big band. (Courtesy Central Business District Foundation.)

BROADWAY STREET LOBBY, 1980s. Aside from the dust, peeling paint, musty carpeting, and a number of nonfunctioning light fixtures, the Broadway Street lobby and storm lobby were usable for the rock concert audience. There was even a bit of limited fluorescent lighting for the stained-glass ceiling. (Courtesy Michigan Opera Theatre.)

BROADWAY LOBBY CANDY COUNTER, 1980s. Grand Circus Live! subcontracted concessions to a third party. The menu was limited to soda, popcorn, and a few popular candy selections. This was a far cry from the venue's movie palace days, when the selection included several brands of soda, Hygrade franks, Everkrisp snacks, a large selection of candy bars, and White Bear Ice Cream. (Courtesy Michigan Opera Theatre.)

A Slightly Tattered Grand Lobby, 1980s. The grand lobby, despite the theater being closed for almost four years, still stood the test of time. The carpeting was frayed and there was peeling paint and missing draperies, but this space was still stunning. Amazingly, the oil paintings and tall brass torchieres were still in place. (Courtesy Michigan Opera Theatre.)

Movie Screen Still in Use During Rock Years, 1980s. The Grand Circus screen was 54 feet wide, one of the largest movie screens in Michigan. During the rock concert years, it was utilized for concert telecasts and productions such as *Beatlemania!* When the theater opened in 1922, the original movie screen was only 20 feet wide and 24 feet high. (Courtesy Michigan Opera Theatre.)

AUDITORIUM AS SEEN FROM THE STAGE, 1980s. Grand Circus Live!, for most productions, utilized the entire main floor and box level for seating. Only for specific concerts were balcony seats sold, as the walls and ceiling in that area had sustained a fair amount of water damage. The old seats from the movie palace days were retained for balcony seating. (Courtesy Michigan Opera Theatre.)

OVERVIEW OF THE BOX LEVEL, 1980s. The box level remained relatively intact. The decorative plaster ceiling, milk glass light fixtures, and mood-lit ceiling cove were still intact. The brass rods and heavy green drapery for privacy in each of the 17 boxes had been removed, and lighting and sound equipment were placed in the center box. (Courtesy Michigan Opera Theatre.)

OVAL CEILING IN THE AUDITORIUM, 1980s. The oval during the movie palace days signified the sky and was painted in several shades of blue. It was surrounded by several thousand pink, yellow, and blue incandescent lightbulbs. During the years of vacancy, the oval and the back walls of the balcony sustained severe water damage. (Courtesy Michigan Opera Theatre.)

AUDITORIUM VIEW FROM THE STAGE, 1980s. This image shows the new seating that was added in 1960 on the main floor and the box level. The balcony seating was a holdover from the 1940s, and many of the seats were unusable. A concession stand had been added outside the door on the far right. Just as in 1922, the auditorium featured six aisles of seats on the main floor, 17 boxes, and four aisles of seats in the balcony. (Courtesy Michigan Opera Theatre.)

CONCERT FLYER FOR THE PLASMATICS, 1982. This concert featuring Wendy O. Williams and the Plasmatics was one of the most controversial of 1982. The punk band was known for its aggressive music and brushes with the law. Local producer Gail Parenteau booked the gig, and well-known local designer Gary Grimshaw created the flyers and posters. (Courtesy Michael Hauser.)

CONCERT FLYER FOR THE B-52'S, 1982. The B-52's sold out two nights at Grand Circus Live! The *Detroit Free Press* referred to the group as "the most effervescent thing from Georgia since Billy Carter!" This stop coincided with their Warner Bros. album *Mesopotamia*, projecting a more mood-induced rhythm and blues sound. The group's name was derived from a slang expression for a bouffant hairdo. (Courtesy Michael Hauser.)

FOLLOWING THE CLOSURE AS A MOVIE PALACE, 1978. When Community Theatres decided to close the venue, they added a veiled message ("Closed Temporarily") on the marquee and boarded up the doors on Broadway and Madison Avenue. By this time, the two attached office buildings were devoid of tenants, and the main-floor businesses had also closed. (Courtesy Walter P. Reuther Library, Wayne State University Archives.)

DEMOLITION BY NEGLECT TOUCH-UP, 1987. As the result of a non-sanctioned public exhibit, Demolition by Neglect, the city was forced to clean up building facades and abandoned structures, many of which it owned. The treatment for the Grand Circus included the addition of canvas canopies over windows, boarded-up sections, and canvas over the decaying marquee. (Courtesy Detroit Free Press Archives.)

Box Level Damage, 1989. Four years of abandonment from 1985 to 1989 caused serious damage to this once-magnificent theater. Plaster damage was abundant, and with no electricity for heating or air-conditioning, it took months to properly air out the venue. (Courtesy Cristina DiChiera.)

Auditorium Side Wall Damage, 1980s. Despite being surrounded by plaster damage and water and ice dripping from the auditorium ceiling, the former pipe organ chamber on the Broadway Street side of the auditorium remained intact. Even the original draperies and chandelier hanging from the lion's mouth were still untouched at this time. (Courtesy Cristina DiChiera.)

AUDITORIUM DAMAGE LOOKING TOWARD LOBBY, 1980s. This forlorn image captures the extent of the plaster damage to the walls, columns, boxes, and balcony. Four years of rain, ice, and snow seeping in from a poorly maintained roof caused considerable damage. The pipes had also frozen shortly following the closure of the theater. (Courtesy Michigan Opera Theatre.)

SURVEYING THE DAMAGE FROM THE STAGE, 1988. Portions of the proscenium arch were lying on the stage, seats were damaged by falling ceiling plaster, and the orchestra pit resembled a lake. The stage floor was so weak that the wood was threadbare in spots, with gaping holes providing a look clear through to the two basement levels. (Courtesy Cristina DiChiera.)

GRAND LOBBY DAMAGE, 1980s. Despite the water damage in the grand lobby, the chandeliers, aside from missing crystals, were spared major damage. It was surmised that these light fixtures were simply too large and difficult to safely remove from the ceiling. (Courtesy Michigan Opera Theatre.)

GRAND STAIRCASE DAMAGE, 1988. This image was taken while there was no electricity in the building. Plaster damage had begun due to a leaking roof, carpeting had been removed, oil paintings were stolen, light fixtures were illegally removed, and piles of trash were everywhere thanks to squatters living in the theater. (Courtesy Michigan Opera Theatre.)

Box Level Damage Leading to Third Level, 1980s. This set of stairs leading from the box level to the third floor was gated off, as it had not been utilized much since the 1970s. As movie attendance declined following the Blaxploitation and kung-fu eras, management attempted to focus seating only in the center section of the main floor. (Courtesy James Luzenski.)

Five

THE HOPEFUL 1990S

LOOKING FORLORN IN THE COLD, 1990. Michigan Opera Theatre purchased the building in 1989 to create the new Detroit Opera House, and embarked upon a $20 million capital campaign to renovate the theater and attached office structures. (Courtesy Michael Hauser.)

THE PARAMOUNT REEMERGES, 1993. During the dismantling of the large Grand Circus marquee, faded history was unveiled. The Paramount logo from 1929 and the Publix logo appeared after having been covered over for almost 60 years. Publix was the theatrical arm of Paramount Pictures at a time when studios were permitted to own theaters and program them with their products for screen and stage. (Courtesy Michael Hauser.)

ADDITIONAL HISTORY UNCOVERED, 1994. When the faux walls were removed in the Madison Avenue lobby, several hand-painted signs were unveiled from the United Detroit Theatres era of ownership. Another sign promoted the fact that the Broadway Capitol had adopted the neighboring Madison Theatre's policy of "2 great hits while they are new, at bargain prices!" (Courtesy Michael Hauser.)

MISGUIDED MARQUEE MESSAGE, 1990. Following a raucous concert featuring Grace Jones in 1985, Grand Circus Live! closed its doors. "Do it in Detroit" was added to the marquee, and the once-glamorous doyenne of Broadway Street sat vacant and open to vandals for the next four years. (Courtesy James Luzenski.)

ILLEGAL ROOFTOP TENANTS, 1990. Since the theater was wide open for all to enter between 1985 and 1989, it attracted its share of scrappers and squatters. This image shows a rooftop apartment complete with lawn chair and shopping cart. In many instances, carts were utilized by scrappers to transport anything of value to waiting taxis. (Courtesy Michael Hauser.)

DISBELIEF IN THE UPPER BALCONY, 1990. The upper balcony of the Grand Circus experienced severe water damage from a faulty roof between 1985 and 1989. The previous owner walked away from the venue without disconnecting the water, and several basements were completely flooded. Additionally, an ill-planned rooftop restaurant left gaping holes in the roof, allowing ice, snow, and rain to penetrate the venue for four years. (Photograph by Santa Fabio, courtesy Michigan Opera Theatre.)

Office Floor Damage, 1989. Offices and showrooms on the upper floors of both the attached Broadway Street and Madison Avenue office towers had emptied out in the 1970s. With no utilities, these floors encountered water damage and vandalism. (Courtesy Michael Hauser.)

Damage in Former Business Library, 1990. Wayne County Community College had leased the former Walsh College of Business space on the fifth and sixth floors of the Madison Avenue office tower in the 1970s as its first home. This image captures the damage in the school's former library. (Courtesy Michael Hauser.)

DREAMING OF REOPENING THE DOORS, 1990s. General director David DiChiera and managing director Kim Johnson lead a group tour of the venue. Robert Dewar, then chairman of the board of Michigan Opera Theatre, on the far left, is surveying the work completed thus far in the auditorium. The first capital campaign was chaired by Philip E. Benton, then president of Ford Motor Company. (Courtesy Michigan Opera Theatre.)

ONE OF MANY GROUP TOURS TO GAIN SUPPORT, 1990s. David DiChiera leads a group of prospective donors through the restoration process of converting the Grand Circus Theatre into the new Detroit Opera House. The early 1990s were a tough economic time, and it took over 50 of these tours before community leaders began to believe in the project. (Photograph by Jerome Magid, courtesy Michigan Opera Theatre.)

DETROIT OPERA HOUSE PARTICIPATES IN SPOTLIGHT TOUR, 1993. Throughout the 1990s, the Grand Circus Park Development Association sponsored well-attended tours of historic structures and lobbies in the district to build awareness of the planned restoration of the new Detroit Opera House and other renovation projects in the downtown area. (Courtesy Michigan Opera Theatre.)

OPERA BALL TO COMMENCE AUDITORIUM RESTORATION, 1994. Michigan Opera Theatre's largest annual fundraiser was the Opera Ball, held each year in a different historic building in Detroit. For 1994, to drive home the need for financial support, MOT held the event in the unrestored theater. Thanks to Ford Motor Company and MOT donors, $250,000 was raised that evening so major restoration work could commence. (Photograph by Jerome Magid, courtesy Michigan Opera Theatre.)

80

Mailing Address:
P.O. Box 32658
Detroit MI 48232

Offices:
2062 Penobscot
Building
Detroit MI 48226

313.961.5880

New performance
Theater

We invite you to attend a theater production unlike any other!

Detroit's internationally acclaimed **Theater Grottesco** returns home to celebrate ten years of artistic madness with their special anniversary engagement, **"The Angels' Cradle."** Filled with urban energy and imagery, this creation is a landmark work speaking to all people.

A story of discovery, humor and **hope**, "The Angels' Cradle" explores the deep humanity of a tiny group of outcasts in the underworld of contemporary, urban society. Transporting a blend of genres and styles from centuries of theater to modern times, the cast **powerfully** communicates their world of isolation with **tears** and laughter. Their confrontation, clash and coming together with a homeless man **speaks** of the undying spirit that springs from our crumbling cities of today.

This unique drama will be **showcased** in the historic Grand Circus Theater, soon to open as the Detroit Opera House in the fall of 1995. Combining the present state of the building's restoration with the nature of their production, Grottesco has set the stage for an absolutely **unforgettable** performance.

A rare experience to be unequaled on any stage the world over, "The Angels' Cradle" premieres with a gala celebration on April 15th, and continues for two consecutive weekends. The gala festivities include a reception and an **afterglow** featuring eating, drinking, dancing and merriment with the cast and crew of this dynamic production. Please come join us for the adventure!

Theater Grottesco has been recognized worldwide for their achievements. Michigan's only professional touring company, they have garnered support from a host of major foundations and corporations. Included in this list is their recent placement in the National Endowment for the Arts Advancement Program Phase One. This NEA program recognizes organizations which have gained national recognition through intense commitment to a unique artistic vision. Theater Grottesco has the distinction and honor of being the only group of artists selected and participating from Michigan.

Printed on recycled paper

THEATRE GROTTESCO PRODUCTION STAGED, 1994. Another means to draw interest to the Detroit Opera House restoration project was to partner with local performance group Theatre Grottesco. Its production of *The Angels' Cradle* was staged for two weeks in the cold, damp confines of the Grand Circus auditorium. Seating was only allowed on the box level per the fire marshal. (Courtesy Michael Hauser.)

DEMOLITION BEGINS FOR NEW STAGE HOUSE, 1993. David and Karen DiChiera are interviewed at the ground-breaking ceremony to construct the new stage house for the Detroit Opera House on June 21, 1993. Besides acquiring the surface parking lot on Broadway Street, MOT also acquired the former eight-story Robert's Furs Building on Madison Avenue, which was demolished for stage expansion. (Photograph by Jerome Magid, courtesy Michigan Opera Theatre.)

RENOVATING THE FOURTH-FLOOR CORRIDOR, 1996. This long corridor runs the entire length of the upper balcony on the fourth floor of the auditorium. The walls featured the original color palette of the theater, and hand-painted frescoes once lined this illuminated gateway to the largest concentration of seating in the theater. (Photograph by Mark Mancinelli, courtesy Michigan Opera Theatre.)

PREPPING THE THIRD FLOOR FOR RESTORATION, 1995. This area is on the third floor of the Broadway Street side of the theater and is today known as the Townsend Lobby. This connecting lobby suffered severe water damage, with entire sections of decorative plaster destroyed as well as the historic mirrors. (Photograph by Mark Mancinelli, courtesy Michigan Opera Theatre.)

DAMAGE TO THE MADISON AVENUE SIDE OF THE SECOND FLOOR, 1995. Damage on this side of the theater consisted of plaster damage, missing light fixtures, and the ladies' powder room being almost completely obliterated save the fireplace and pagodas atop two large decorative mirrors. (Photograph by Mark Mancinelli, courtesy Michigan Opera Theatre.)

PREPARING THE BOX LEVEL FOR RESTORATION, 1995. The box seating area on the second floor suffered extensive water damage. Decorative plaster and elaborate light fixtures were destroyed. As part of the fundraising campaign, MOT sold naming rights for each of the 17 boxes to major corporations and foundations. This was a major boost to jump-start full-scale restoration of the theater in 1994. (Photograph by Mark Mancinelli, courtesy Michigan Opera Theatre.)

AUDITORIUM EXPOSED TO THE GREAT OUTDOORS, 1995. This image shows work proceeding on restoration of the proscenium arch while construction of the new stage house continued now that the wall behind the former movie screen had been dismantled. (Photograph by Mark Mancinelli, courtesy Michigan Opera Theatre.)

ORIGINAL STEEL GIRDERS EXPOSED, 1995. This area is the Townsend Lobby on the third floor of the Broadway Street side of the theater. Due to deterioration of the plaster walls, the original steel girders from 1922 can be seen. (Photograph by Mark Mancinelli, courtesy Michigan Opera Theatre.)

STAGE HOUSE ADDITION CONSTRUCTION BEGINS, 1995. Once the Robert's Furs Building was demolished and the adjacent surface parking lot cleared, construction began on the new 75,000-square-foot stage house behind the proscenium arch. The large opening is where the movie screen was previously situated. (Courtesy Michigan Opera Theatre.)

STAGE HOUSE CONSTRUCTION PROGRESS, 1995. Scaffolding was now in place for plaster restoration in the auditorium while concrete was poured for the stage house addition. The new stage would be 65 feet deep for production purposes and 90 feet deep overall. It would be 110 feet wide and 85 feet high. (Courtesy Michigan Opera Theatre.)

STRUCTURAL STEEL RISES FOR NEW STAGE HOUSE, 1995. The new stage has 89 line sets, allowing scenery, scrims, and lighting to be raised out of sight and lowered into position. The stage floor contains several trap doors to lower or raise artists to and from the stage. (Courtesy Michigan Opera Theatre.)

FINAL EXTERIOR TOUCHES TO STAGE HOUSE, 1995. Scaffolding is almost ready to be removed, exposing the contemporary exterior of the stage house facing Grand Circus Park. The stage house also features a large freight elevator; a dock to accommodate two tractor trailers; star, maestro, and chorus dressing rooms; a rehearsal studio 50 feet above the back portion of the stage; a musician's room; and piano storage. (Courtesy Michigan Opera Theatre.)

TYPICAL DAMAGE THROUGHOUT THE VENUE, 1995. This image shows a major crack in one of the main floor decorative columns. Water seepage and the lack of heat or air for four years played havoc on plaster surfaces throughout the theater. (Photograph by Mark Mancinelli, Courtesy Michigan Opera Theatre.)

THE HAUNTED LOOK OF THE GRAND LOBBY, 1990. The temporary shop lights provide a stark look to the grand lobby prior to the actual restoration phase of the theater. The carpeting had been removed, crystals removed from the chandeliers, and the roof stabilized to prevent further moisture damage. (Photograph by Santa Fabio, Courtesy Michigan Opera Theatre.)

RESTORATION OF THE FORD LOBBY LOOKING TOWARD BROADWAY STREET, 1996. During the four years of abandonment, the stained-glass ceiling and chandelier were stolen, and there was considerable plaster damage to the walls and a portion of the ceiling as well as decorative plaster bordering the box office. (Photograph by Mark Mancinelli, Courtesy Michigan Opera Theatre.)

RESTORATION OF FORD LOBBY, LOOKING TOWARD GRAND LOBBY, 1996. A 1998 grant from the Ford Motor Company Fund allowed for the completion of this lobby that included decorative painting, installing a faithful reproduction of the original stained-glass ceiling, and restoring a chandelier that is similar to what was originally installed in 1922. (Photograph by Mark Mancinelli, Courtesy Michigan Opera Theatre.)

RESTORATION OF BROADWAY STREET STORM LOBBY, 1996. This area sustained ceiling damage, a portion of the box office had been obliterated, and decorative cast iron had been chiseled away by scrappers. In his design for this theater, C. Howard Crane's plan was to create lobby spaces to beguile guests with the elegance and beauty of a European opera house. (Photograph by Mark Mancinelli, courtesy Michigan Opera Theatre.)

PLASTER RESTORATION DEMONSTRATION FOR THE MEDIA, 1995. Chris Richardson, foreman for Plasterers Local 67, demonstrates the intricacies of creating plaster molds for various restoration areas of the new Detroit Opera House. Richardson, in another life in the United Kingdom, had created plaster models for a number of films, including *Superman*, *Star Wars*, and *Moonraker*. Locally, he also worked on the restoration of the state capitol and the Wayne County Building. (Courtesy Michigan Opera Theatre.)

COMMERCIAL INTERIOR SYSTEMS CREW CREATING PLASTER CASTINGS, 1995. An estimated 85 percent of the theater's plasterwork, much of it in decorative arches, moldings, domes, and friezes, needed repair or replacement when the restoration project at the new Detroit Opera House began. At its peak, there were 22 plasterers on site, some from as far away as Cincinnati, Lansing, and Jackson. (Courtesy Michigan Opera Theatre.)

THE RARE ARTFORM OF WET PLASTERING, 1995. Wet plastering is out of favor, as today's construction tends to utilize drywall. This plasterer is working on a delicate design on the ceiling of the auditorium. The proscenium arch around the stage featured 23 large panels, at 800 pounds each, that also needed to be restored and recast. (Photograph by Mark Mancinelli, courtesy Michigan Opera Theatre.)

INTRICATE UNITS OF DECORATIVE PLASTER MOLDS, 1995. The plaster shops were set up in what is today the Cadillac Café, with an outpost in the center of the auditorium. Here master craftsmen recreated molds for various sections of the theater. This image shows various decorative molds for ceilings and walls. (Photograph by Mark Mancinelli, courtesy Michigan Opera Theatre.)

GRAND LOBBY DECORATIVE PAINTING, 1997. Upon opening in 1996, plaster restoration in the grand lobby was completed. However, decorative painting did not commence until 1997 thanks to an anonymous gift. Eugenio Painting Company of Grosse Pointe Woods, Michigan, employed a staff of 22 artisans from Ukraine to complete decorative painting and create 28 allegorical murals on canvas. (Courtesy Michigan Opera Theatre.)

BIRD'S-EYE VIEW OF GRAND LOBBY RESTORATION, 1996. A crew can be seen here prepping walls for a base coat of primer. Another team had worked on plaster repair and yet another crew on reproducing the murals on canvas, which had badly deteriorated due to water damage and dry rot. Originally all of the murals were frescoes painted directly onto the plaster surfaces. (Photograph by Mark Mancinelli, courtesy Michigan Opera Theatre.)

Seat Installation Begins, 1996. Renovating this venue into the new Detroit Opera House, the seating capacity was reduced from almost 4,000 to 2,700. The seating contractor was Greenville, Michigan–based Country Roads, later absorbed into Irwin Seating. The seat fabric is not traditional upholstery but automotive upholstery, which is thicker, more durable, and absorbs sound better. (Photograph by Mark Mancinelli, courtesy Michigan Opera Theatre.)

Sets Arriving for the Opening Production, 1996. With ongoing restoration still underway, the sets for Puccini's *La Bohème* arrived and the stage hands began to assemble the various acts of the production. Looking out into the auditorium, one can also view the completion of seat installation. (Photograph by Mark Mancinelli, courtesy Michigan Opera Theatre.)

IT TOOK A VILLAGE TO COMPLETE, 1996. This image includes a fraction of the over 300 men and women who labored for two years to restore what would become the Detroit Opera House. Painters, plasterers, plumbers, electricians, stagehands, and riggers were among the skilled craftspeople, tradesmen, and technicians needed to complete the renovation and restoration. (Photograph by Alan Lessig, courtesy the *Detroit News*.)

OVERVIEW OF THE AUDITORIUM, 1996. Despite the doors opening in 1996, there was still much work to accomplish in the following years, such as additional decorative painting, applying historically accurate wallpaper to the side walls in the balcony, applying decorative paint to the grand lobby, renovating what would become the donor lounge, and refurbishing what would become the boutique. (Courtesy Michigan Opera Theatre.)

OFFICIAL RIBBON CUTTING, 1996. The opening of the Detroit Opera House included the ribbon cutting with (from left to right) Robert Dewar, chairman of the board of MOT; Dame Joan Sutherland; and David DiChiera, general director of MOT. The evening commenced with 14 celebrated singers, 70 musicians, and 2 conductors. (Courtesy Michigan Opera Theatre.)

GUESTS ARRIVE FOR THE GALA OPENING, 1996. Sunday, April 21, 1996, was the afternoon when the new Detroit Opera House was officially christened. After seven years of capital campaigns to raise necessary funding for the restoration, renovation, and move to this venue, the big night had finally arrived. (Courtesy Michigan Opera Theatre.)

OVERVIEW OF DETROIT OPERA HOUSE CAMPUS, 1996. The renovation of the new Detroit Opera House paved the way for the surrounding neighborhood to rejuvenate itself. As a result of the investment the Detroit Opera House made, restaurants opened and residences followed, as did hotels, the Boll YMCA, Comerica Park for professional baseball, and Ford Field for professional football. (Courtesy Michigan Opera Theatre.)

LUCIANO PAVAROTTI RAISES A TOAST, 1996. With Pavarotti and a star-studded cast of world-renowned artists, the Detroit Opera House opened its doors on the anniversary of the 25th season of Michigan Opera Theatre. It was a triumphant event and fulfilled David DiChiera's dream to give Detroit a true opera house. (Courtesy Michigan Opera Theatre.)

LUCIANO PAVAROTTI AND DAVID DICHIERA BACKSTAGE, 1996. Pavarotti first stepped foot in what would become the new Detroit Opera House in 1991 following an appearance at Joe Louis Arena. He tested his pipes in the abandoned theater and blessed the acoustics by stating, "Yes, I think this will be a very nice opera house. I will come when it is completed." He kept his word, returning not only for the opening but for three additional MOT fundraisers. (Photograph by Mark Mancinelli, courtesy Michigan Opera Theatre.)

LOADING IN SETS FOR *LA BOHÈME*, 1996. Just six days following the opening gala, Michigan Opera Theatre celebrated its silver anniversary by opening Puccini's *La Bohème*, its first opera on the stage of its new home at the Detroit Opera House. It was a brilliant choice—an opera about love and death and an unabashed passion for life. (Photograph by Mark Mancinelli, courtesy Michigan Opera Theatre.)

AT LAST, THE CURTAIN RISES ON A NEW ERA, 1996. The opening of the Detroit Opera House not only provided Michigan Opera Theatre a permanent home but also created an opportunity for the company to grow. Factors such as flexibility with scheduling, rehearsal space within the theater, and the incredible size of the stage and orchestra pit positioned the company for a new era. (Courtesy Michigan Opera Theatre.)

NOT QUITE AT THE FINISH LINE, 1996. From left to right, Robert Dewar, chairman of the MOT board; David DiChiera, MOT founder and general director; and Kim Johnson, MOT managing director, relax with a sigh of relief that the facility can finally be "operable." Johnson stated that the biggest challenge was to change the public's perceptions about the project and about Downtown Detroit. (Photograph by Mark Mancinelli, courtesy Michigan Opera Theatre.)

A NORTH AMERICAN PREMIERE, 1999. In 1999, Michigan Opera Theatre presented three extraordinary premieres by staging Massenet's *Werther* at the Detroit Opera House. It was Italian singing sensation tenor Andrea Bocelli's North American opera debut, the company debut of *Werther*, and mezzo-soprano Denyce Graves's MOT debut. (Photograph by Mark Mancinelli, courtesy Michigan Opera Theatre.)

RENOVATED OFFICE SPACE IN MADISON AVENUE TOWER, 1998. The various floors in the Madison Avenue office tower became the home of MOT in 1998. Pictured here is the fifth-floor home of marketing and development. Many of the floors feature a post-deconstructionist look, with exposed brick walls and ceilings and reclaimed decorative glass from C. Howard Crane's architectural offices. (Courtesy Albert Kahn Associates Architects & Engineers.)

FRANKEL DONOR LOUNGE, 1997. The former retail space on the second floor of the Madison Avenue office tower was renovated in 1997 thanks to the generosity and support of Barbara and Herman Frankel. The architecture in this donor lounge encompasses themes from Frank Lloyd Wright, Charles Rennie McIntosh, and the Art Deco era. Amenities also include nicely appointed restrooms, a beverage bar, and a full-service kitchen. (Courtesy Albert Kahn Associates Architects & Engineers.)

Six

THE HOMEWARD-BOUND 2000s

AN ICON IN THE NEIGHBORHOOD, 2005. By the 2000s, the Detroit Opera House came into its own with 300,000 guests a year for opera, dance, Broadway, graduations, weddings, and business meetings. The building also became an important canvas to advertise special events, such as this Chevrolet banner promoting the Major League Baseball All-Star Game at Comerica Park. (Courtesy Michel Hauser.)

MARSHALL FIELD'S SPONSORED PRODUCTION, 2001. Marshall Field's, under the auspices of owner Target Corporation and its Project Imagine community involvement program, sponsored a production of *The Marriage of Figaro* that included a large lobby display of the history of the store's bridal registry, floral arrangements in the lobby, photo ops, and complimentary samples of Frango chocolates. (Courtesy Jeff Garland Photography.)

THE GLORIOUS SPLENDOR OF THE RESTORED AUDITORIUM, 2000. Albert Kahn Collaborative, the architects for the restoration of the original theater portion of the new Detroit Opera House project, commissioned architectural conservation specialist Steve Seebohm, who microscopically examined over 750 paint chips from throughout the venue to reproduce the original 1922 color palette. (Courtesy Albert Kahn Associates Architects & Engineers.)

A VIEW OF THE RESTORED GRAND LOBBY, 2000. Eugenio Painting Company, a multigenerational firm in Grosse Pointe Woods, utilized Sherwin Williams paints that were specially made to replicate the taupes, blues, deep reds, and metallic bronzes of the original theater. Albert Kahn Collaborative received a national award for excellence in outstanding interiors for this project from the American Institute of Architects. (Courtesy Glen Calvin Moon Photography.)

RESTORED GRAND STAIRCASE BANISTER, 2000. The banister leading guests to the top of the grand staircase features cast iron rosettes, cornucopias of fruit, and the Capitol crest. All incorporate the Capitol's original color palette. The deep walnut railings were stripped and revarnished. The carpeting in the grand lobby is a replica of original carpeting found in the upper balcony and produced by Durkan Mills. (Courtesy Albert Kahn Associates Architects & Engineers.)

OVERVIEW OF THE EXPANDED STAGE, 2000. The stage of the new Detroit Opera House is the largest in Michigan and one of the largest between New York and Chicago. The main floor of the stage is 7,000 square feet. The fly loft is 85 feet high and 110 feet wide and is capable of holding 89 line sets for scenery, scrims, or lighting. The orchestra pit contains two horizontal mechanical platform lifts that can be raised and lowered separately and can accommodate 90 musicians. (Courtesy Albert Kahn Associates Architects &Engineers.)

RESTORING THE LOBBY CEILING ON THE THIRD FLOOR, 2002. College for Creative Studies faculty member Roumen Boudev spent eight months on scaffolding painting murals on the ceiling of the Townsend Lobby on the Broadway Street side of the theater. To prep the lobby for painting, the ceiling had to be hand sanded using dry fresco techniques and primed with gesso. (Courtesy Michael Hauser.)

ASSISTING ROUMEN ON LOBBY MURALS, 2002. Beverly Hall Smith, also a College for Creative Studies faculty member, assisted Boudev with the restoration of this lobby, which consisted of an intricate design featuring the portraits of six composers interspersed between four medallions that feature scenes from operas and ballets. The center of the ceiling is a large floral pattern with a surrounding border with gold gilt trim. (Courtesy Michael Hauser.)

THE RESTORED BOX LEVEL, 1998. There are 17 boxes today, just as there were when the theater opened in 1922. As part of the initial capital campaign, each box was sold for $250,000 to major corporations and foundations. The box doors feature their names, and they have first choice of seats for all productions. (Courtesy Albert Kahn Associates Architects & Engineers.)

EXTERIOR TERRA COTTA RESTORATION, 2002. The Broadway Street side of the theater and office tower suffered considerable damage during the abandoned years. This side of the complex is adorned with beautiful terra cotta, which is hardened clay covered with several layers of glaze and adhered to the structure by conduit. Detroit's freeze/thaw cycle in the winter caused major portions of terra cotta to crack and fall off. (Courtesy Michael Hauser.)

TERRA COTTA RESTORATION, 2002. Local contractor Grunwell Cashero Company worked with Boston Valley Terra Cotta of Orchard Park, New York, to restore and recreate new molds for the Broadway side of the venue. Over the course of two years, entire swaths of the structure were loaded onto flatbeds and trucked to Boston Valley, where engineers determined what could be salvaged and what could be recast. (Courtesy Michael Hauser.)

TERRA COTTA RESTORATION COMPLETE, 2002. This view showcases the restored exterior of the Broadway Street facade of the Detroit Opera House. All of the terra cotta tracery was restored and cleaned, new molds were created for the capitals, new windows were installed, and marble panels were restored and cleaned. (Courtesy Jeff Garland Photography.)

GENERAL MOTORS CADILLAC CAFÉ OPENS, 2002. In 2002, Michigan Opera Theatre opened the Cadillac Café in the former retail space on the main floor of the Madison Avenue office tower. This cozy, 80-seat bistro affords guests a place to dine prior to productions and also features a fully stocked bar. McIntosh Poris Architects were responsible for the renovation of this unique space. (Courtesy Jeff Garland Photography.)

A New Tradition Is Born, 2002. Conducted by MOT assistant music director and chorus master Suzanne Mallare Acton, *Too Hot to Handel* has been a Detroit Opera House and Rackham Choir tradition since 2002. Each year, thousands enjoy this jazz/gospel version of Handel's *The Messiah*. The production features 85 members of the Rackham Choir and members of the MOT Orchestra. Tenor Rod Dixon is pictured here. (Courtesy Michigan Opera Theatre.)

MOT Purchases Shopper's Parking Garage, 2003. Hudson's Department Store had demolished its 1939 garage on this block of Broadway Street in 1950 to construct the facility seen here. The new garage featured parking for 850 vehicles on five floors and had ground-floor retail space for 14 tenants. By the 2000s, following several different owners, the facility had deteriorated and was available for purchase. (Courtesy Central Business District Foundation.)

New Opera House Parking Center Opens, 2005. With the opening of Comerica Park and Ford Field for professional sports teams, parking for patrons of the new Detroit Opera House became a challenge, and the Michigan Opera Theatre Board of Directors, led by Herman Frankel, strongly suggested a remedy. As a result, the former Hudson's Department Store garage was purchased and demolished. In its place, a state-of-the-art 780-vehicle garage was constructed with an attached office building for additional revenue. (Courtesy Michael Hauser.)

MOT ALLESEE OPERA AND DANCE LIBRARY, 2006. This resource center on the second floor of the Broadway Street office tower is the official library for Michigan Opera Theatre and the Detroit Opera House. Funded with a generous gift from Maggie and Robert Allesee, amenities include books, scores, CDs, videos, and hundreds of unique items from MOT productions such as performance reviews, photographs, playbills, and recordings. (Courtesy Mitty Carter Photography.)

MOT COSTUME SHOP, 2006. This was a project funded by Lee and Floy Barthel. The goal was to locate the shop in an area on the third floor of the Broadway Street office tower where there was plenty of natural light, adding updated sewing machines, a fitting area, and a comfortable floor for those associates designing and cutting patterns. The soft, comfortable floor in this area is manufactured from recycled tires. (Courtesy Mitty Carter Photography.)

MARGO V. COHEN CENTER FOR DANCE, 2006. Located on the fifth floor of the Ford Center for Arts and Learning, this studio is a component of MOT's Community Outreach program. The center hosts a popular dance film series, a summer dance intensive program, and year-round classes from beginning to advanced dance students. (Courtesy Mitty Carter Photography.)

CHRYSLER BLACK BOX THEATRE, 2018. This flexible performance space opened in 2006 on the sixth floor of the Ford Center for Arts and Learning thanks to a generous gift from Chrysler Corporation. Seating can be arranged in a myriad of ways, from classroom style to risers. The room features overhead lighting and a screen for films and can easily be converted to a dance studio. Besides productions and rehearsals, the room is used for business meetings, luncheons, and classes. (Courtesy Mitty Carter Photography.)

FIRST WORLD PREMIERE FOR THE DETROIT OPERA HOUSE, 2005. On May 7, 2005, all eyes were on the Detroit Opera House as the curtain ascended on the highly anticipated world premiere of *Margaret Garner*, featuring mezzo-soprano Denyce Graves and bass baritone Gregg Baker. This landmark collaboration between Nobel Prize–winning author Toni Morrison and Grammy Award–winning composer Richard Danielpour was the result of David DiChiera's desire to present a culturally relevant American work as MOT's first world premiere on the Detroit Opera House stage. (Photograph by John Grigaitis, courtesy Michigan Opera Theatre.)

ANOTHER MOMENTOUS WORLD PREMIERE, 2007. With a great deal of pride, MOT commenced its 37th season with the highly anticipated world premiere of David DiChiera's opera *Cyrano*, featuring soprano Leah Partridge and baritone Marian Pop. This landmark premiere at the Detroit Opera House catapulted the composer and the opera company he founded into the international spotlight, garnering audience favor and critical acclaim from around the world. (Photograph by John Grigaitis, courtesy Michigan Opera Theatre.)

Major Dance Companies at the Detroit Opera House. MOT announced the addition of a dance series in 1996, presenting the long-awaited return of American Ballet Theatre (pictured). Since then, the Opera House stage has hosted Alvin Ailey American Dance Theater, the Bolshoi, Dance Theatre of Harlem, Ballet Hispanico, the Joffrey, the Kirov, and more. The Detroit Opera House also became the home of Michigan's largest production of *The Nutcracker*, featuring the MOT Orchestra. (Photograph by John Grigaitis, courtesy Michigan Opera Theatre.)

Opera House Sky Deck Opens, 2013. MOT supporters Lee and Floy Barthel provided a gift that literally paved the way for one of Detroit's hidden gems to open in 2013. This rooftop space, spanning almost 10,000 square feet, has become a popular location for unforgettable weddings and special events with incredible 360-degree views of Downtown Detroit. (Courtesy Mitty Carter Photography.)

BROADWAY IN DETROIT PARTNERSHIP, 2007. The Detroit Opera House and Broadway in Detroit entered into a landmark partnership to bring large-scale touring Broadway productions to the Detroit Opera House. The first production was Disney's six-week run of *The Lion King*, which was enjoyed by more than 120,000 guests. (Courtesy Broadway in Detroit.)

KIDS NIGHT ON BROADWAY, 2018. The 2018 holiday season saw 95,000 guests enjoy the wonderment of Disney's *Aladdin*. Collectively, over one million patrons have been enthralled by Broadway in Detroit presentations on the stage of the Detroit Opera House. At the same time, guests are exposed to the Detroit Opera House and its offerings. (Courtesy Broadway in Detroit.)

CENTER STAGE WEDDINGS, 2000s. From walking down the aisle to the last dance, wedding ceremonies have become a time-honored tradition at the Detroit Opera House. Ceremonies and rehearsal dinners have been staged in lounges, on the great stage, and in the lobbies. Bridal party photographs on the grand staircase are a must. (Courtesy Continental Dining Management.)

MEMORABLE CORPORATE EVENTS, 2000s. The restored Detroit Opera House has hosted legendary events from auto reveals to stockholders' meetings, TEDx, Crain's Homecoming, and book signings. It has even starred in several major studio films. Guests enjoy one-of-a-kind 21st-century experiences in a dynamic location, whether it is a large event or an intimate gathering. (Courtesy Continental Dining Management.)

Seven

TENANTS THROUGH THE YEARS

Hall's Permanent Waves
Look So Natural
Bobbed Hair, Entire Head $15.00
Don't be without one for the holiday season. Our Nestle Lanoil system of permanent waving given by our expert operators, will give you a permanent wave that snow, rain, shampooing or bath will not effect.

French Natural Part Transformations
Special Price $27.50

HALL'S HAIR SHOP
210 Capitol Theatre Bldg.   1550 Broadway   Main 8735
Open Monday, Tuesday and Friday Evenings

DIVERSE ROSTER OF TENANTS THROUGH THE YEARS, 1920s. From the 1920s through the 1960s, the two office towers attached to the theater were virtually a city-within-a-city. Within these confines, one could watch a movie, enjoy a cocktail, visit a doctor, take a class, purchase a pair of shoes or a fur, get a haircut, and get one's back cracked. Interestingly, at one time, both office towers included 21 beauty salons. (Courtesy Michael Hauser.)

MADISON AVENUE OFFICE TOWER TENANTS, 1929. The Madison Avenue side of the theater housed an array of tenants that included the Tracy Shoppe women's fashions, Talo men's tailor, Curt Wunderlich violin maker, and Jules Schubot Jewelers. Schubot created upscale custom jewelry for well-known clients that included Henry Ford, Tony Martin, Frank Sinatra, and Joan Crawford. (Courtesy Manning Brothers Historical Collection.)

BROADWAY STREET OFFICE TENANTS, 1940. Sidney Krandall, founder of this iconic local jeweler, was the son of a Russian immigrant and watch repair specialist and was one of the original tenants of the Broadway Street tower when the theater opened in 1922. Joined by his sons, Krandall expanded into international mining and, in the late 1950s, moved the business to Highland Park. Additional tenants included the Goody Nut Shop, Cancellations Shoes, and the Haunted Book Shop. (Courtesy Manning Brothers Historical Collection.)

WALSH COLLEGE OF BUSINESS, 1940S. The longest tenant in the Broadway Capitol complex of buildings was Walsh College of Business, which occupied space on the fifth and sixth floors of the Madison Avenue office tower from 1922 to 1970. Walsh began humbly with classes in just two rooms serving 23 students. (Courtesy Walsh College.)

WALSH COLLEGE OF BUSINESS STUDENT LIBRARY, 1930S. By the late 1930s, a study room was created on the sixth floor for students and to house the growing reference collection. The "think" sign at the window in this image was a reminder to students that Walsh wanted its students to work and not speak. Student attire at this time was very businesslike: men wore suits, and women wore dresses. (Courtesy Walsh College.)

WALSH COLLEGE OF BUSINESS CLASS OVERVIEW, 1940s. Early classes were almost exclusively male, with only a few female students, and classes were only conducted in the evening. By 1928, almost 300 students were enrolled, paying a flat fee of $60 for a 17-week semester. Tuition could be divided into three payments of $20 each. Day classes were introduced in 1931. (Courtesy Walsh College.)

POSTWAR GROWTH AT WALSH COLLEGE, 1960s. By 1940, over 700 students had enrolled in classes, but World War II affected enrollment. Walsh taught accounting for the US Army, resulting in a jump to 1,200 students. More women in later years also pursued business careers, providing a need for expansion. With little affordable space downtown, Walsh moved to Troy, Michigan, in 1970 and subleased its space to Wayne County Community College. (Courtesy Walsh College.)

Early Tenant Furs by Robert Ad, 1935. This company was a manufacturing furrier that operated its own retail shops. The first location was in the 1930s on the fifth and sixth floors of the Broadway Street office tower. In 1963, Robert's expanded to the former Dennedy Building, adjacent to the Madison Avenue office tower, and remained there until 1993, when that structure was demolished for the Detroit Opera House stage expansion. (Courtesy Michael Hauser.)

ROBERT'S LATEST CREATION
...THIS SWAGGER BACK

Russian
Caracul
Cape

Lustre Caracul of dark shining splendor—mounted with a luxurious collar of superb silver fox—typifying the truly magnificent fur collection by ROBERT.

A Robert fur coat or cape means the possession of luxurious supple skins deftly manipulated into individual designs, with ultimate in details rarely if ever found in the usual collection of fur coats.

FURS ᵇʸ ROBERT
CAPITOL THEATER BUILDING
1550 BROADWAY

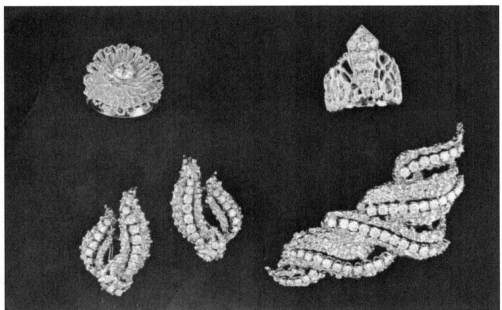

Greenstone's Jewelry Postcard, 1950s. This venerable jeweler was founded by Abraham Greenstone in 1925 in the Broadway Street office tower. Sons Herbert and Irving joined their father in the 1930s and moved the retailer to the nearby Metropolitan Building. In 1949, Greenstone's moved back to the Broadway Capitol, where it remained for the next 20 years. Later locations included the Fisher Building, the Avenue of Fashion, and Birmingham, Michigan, where the company is presently located. (Courtesy Greenstone's Jewelry.)

DISCOVER THOUSANDS OF LOCAL HISTORY BOOKS
FEATURING MILLIONS OF VINTAGE IMAGES

Arcadia Publishing, the leading local history publisher in the United States, is committed to making history accessible and meaningful through publishing books that celebrate and preserve the heritage of America's people and places.

Find more books like this at
www.arcadiapublishing.com

Search for your hometown history, your old stomping grounds, and even your favorite sports team.

CPSIA information can be obtained
at www.ICGtesting.com
Printed in the USA
LVHW081318250222
711812LV00023B/52